£5.99
UK only

Written and edited by Brenda Apsley
Stories adapted from original scripts by Ian Carney, James Henry,
Simon Jowett, Ben Randall and Di Redmond
Designed by Sally Metcalfe

Based upon the television series **Bob the Builder** © HIT Entertainment PLC
and Keith Chapman 2001
With thanks to HOT Animation
Text and illustrations © HIT Entertainment PLC, 2001

www.bobthebuilder.com

Published in Great Britain in 2001 by Egmont World,
an imprint of Egmont Children's Books Limited,
239 Kensington High Street, London W8 6SA

Printed in Italy
ISBN 0 7498 5146 5

Contents

Meet My Team

"Hello, and welcome to my new annual. My name's **Bob**, and I do all sorts of building work. But I can't do it on my own. Luckily, I have a great team to help me. You can meet some of them on these pages."

"I love my cat, **Pilchard**. She likes eating, sleeping and watching TV! She tries to talk, and sometimes I don't think she believes she's a cat at all!"

"I'm **Wendy**, and I'm Bob's business partner. Like Bob, I do all sorts of building work. You can read about the trouble I had with a painting job I did at the farm on page 46."

"Hello. I'm **Scoop**, and I'm a digger dumper, the leader of Bob's team of machines. On page 12 you can read about when I tried to fit a very odd jigsaw puzzle together. It was a lot harder than it looked!"

"Hi, I'm **Roley**, and I'm a steamroller. I love rock and roll music, so it was so cool when I met the singer from my favourite band. You can read all about it on page 32. My friend, **Bird**, talks in whistles, but I know what he is saying."

"Hello, my name is … er … **Lofty**, and I'm a mobile crane. I'm a bit scared of mice, but when I met some recently, luckily they were more interested in Spud! You can read the story on page 46."

"I'm **Muck**, and I love being mucky, so when Wendy set off to do some painting at the farm on her day off, I went with her, because there's lots of lovely messy mud there! You can find out what happened on page 12."

"Hi, I'm **Dizzy**. I'm a cement mixer, but one day Bob had a new job for me. Turn to page 46 to read about the time when I tried to keep Squawk the crow off some wet cement."

"Hee! Hee! I'm **Spud**, and I'm a scarecrow. I like having fun, playing jokes and tricks on people. You can read about what happened when I dressed up as a ghost on page 24."

"This is Scruffty. He's lots of fun, but he always seems to get himself into scrapes! And he's always getting muddy, so I need to bath him a lot!"

"Scruffty yaps a lot to get my attention, and just to let everyone know that he's happy, too."

Yap! Yap!

"I never let Scruffty leave the farm unless he's on a lead, but he's good at escaping – VERY good! And he's VERY hard to catch!"

"Scruffty loves to ride into town on Travis's trailer, especially when Travis goes fast."

Ruff!

"Scruffty would love to play with Pilchard all the time, but often she's too busy napping. But when they do play together, they have a really good time."

Watercolour Wendy

"When I had a day off I planned a quiet time painting. But when Scruffty appeared, my day was far from quiet!"

Bob and the team were getting ready to go off on a job when Wendy came out of the office. "Are you coming to help us, Wendy?" asked Scoop.

"Not today," said Wendy. "It's my day off. I'm going to do some painting at Farmer Pickles's farm."

"Ooo, I love the farm," said Muck. "There's lots and lots of lovely mud there. Can I carry your painting things for you?"

Wendy laughed and put her things in Muck's front digger. "All right," she said. "Have a good day, everyone!"

"You, too!" said Bob, as he left the yard with Scoop, Lofty and Dizzy.

Bob met Mr Bentley in the Town Square. "What's the job for us today, Mr Bentley?" asked Bob.

"I want you to lay these paving stones," said Mr Bentley. "They fit together to make a picture of the town's coat of arms. Look, there's a bird, a tree, a flower and a hammer. I'll leave you to it!"

"Mmm, this could be tricky," said Bob when Mr Bentley had left.

"It's a bit like a big jigsaw puzzle," said Scoop.

"Yes," said Bob, looking at the first stone. "This looks like a corner piece. Lift it into place, please, Lofty."

Just then Mr Bentley came running back.

"OK," said Bob. "Take a break, and we'll finish this when I get back," he told the machines.

But Dizzy, Lofty and Scoop soon got fed up of waiting for Bob.

"I know," said Scoop. "Let's finish the coat of arms ourselves!"

"Brilliant!" cried Dizzy.

But fitting the stones together was very difficult. Their first try was wrong – and so was their second.

"Let's start again!" said Scoop.

At the farm, Wendy got her painting things ready. She told Muck he could stay and watch as long as he was quiet.

But Muck wasn't quiet for long, because along came Scruffty.

"**Woof, woof, woof!**" said Scruffty.

"**Woof, woof, woof!**" replied Muck, laughing.

Scruffty chased around, and so did Muck. Then Scruffty knocked over Wendy's water jar – and ran off with her mobile phone in his mouth!

"Oh, no! Scruffty!" called Wendy, running after him. "Come on, Muck!"

When Wendy and Muck caught up with Scruffty, he didn't have the phone.

"Look at the mud on his nose," said Wendy. "I think he's buried it!"

"Now show Wendy where you buried the phone ..." Muck coaxed.

Scruffty ran off and nudged his nose against the muddy ground. "**Woof, woof!**"

Muck was pleased to have an excuse to dig in the gooey mud. "Muck to the rescue!" he said, and he began to dig.

Muck had dug a deep hole when Farmer Pickles arrived, but there was no sign of Wendy's phone!

"You naughty dog!" said Farmer Pickles when he heard about the missing phone. "Don't worry, Wendy. I'll find it."

He took a bone from his pocket and threw it to Scruffty.

"Ruff, ruff!" barked Scruffty as he ran off with the bone in his mouth. Then he started to dig.

"This must be his place for burying bones," said Farmer Pickles. "Yes, here's your phone, Wendy."

"Oh, thank you, Farmer Pickles!" said Wendy.

Scruffty lifted up his paw to Wendy and whimpered.

"He's saying sorry!" said Muck.

"It's OK, Scruffty," said Wendy, then she had an idea.

"Can I borrow Scruffty for a while?" she asked Farmer Pickles.

"Of course you can," said Farmer Pickles.

Bob returned to the square with Mr Bentley.

"What's been going on?" he said when he saw the stones in the wrong places.

"Jigsaw puzzles are very hard!" said Dizzy.

Bob laughed. "Yes, you have to look at the picture on the lid of the jigsaw box to make sure the pieces are in the right places."

"But we haven't got a box," said Lofty.

"I know," said Bob, and he pointed to the clock tower. "But you can copy the coat of arms on the clock tower. Look, there it is."

"Can we build it?" asked Scoop.

"Yes we can!" said the others.

"Er … yeah, I think so," said Lofty.

The paving stones were soon in the right places, and Bob and the team went back to the yard where they met Wendy and Muck.

Wendy showed Bob her painting. It was Scruffty, with her phone in his mouth!

"That's great," said Bob. "It looks just like Scruffty!"

Then they all heard, "**Woof! Woof!**"

"It sounds like Scruffty!" said Wendy. "But where is he?"

Just then, Scruffty's head popped up from inside Muck's dumper.

"Scruffty wanted to see what everyone thought of his picture," said Muck.

"**Woof!**" barked Scruffty, and everyone laughed.

Bones and Phones

"Scruffty got his bones and phones mixed up, didn't he? He always buries his bones – so he buried my phone, too!"

woof

woof woof!

"Look at the picture very carefully. How many of Scruffty's bones can you find? Can you see where my phone is hidden?"

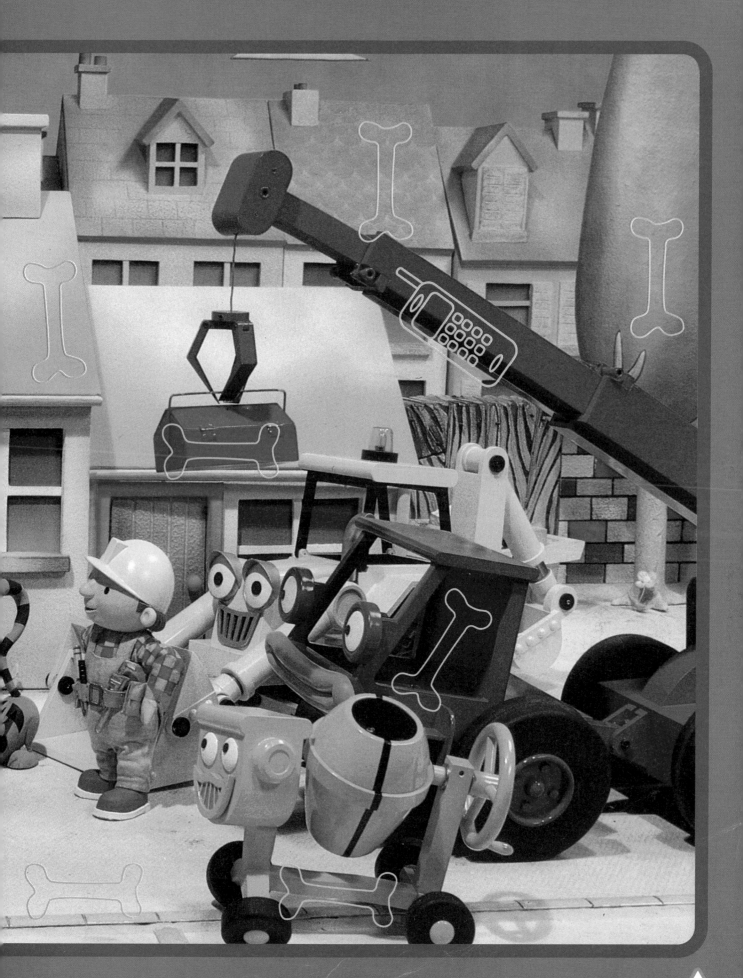

Home Sweet Home

"Read this story and say the names of the pictures for the missing words."

 and are going to dig up an old tree.

Bob   Lofty

They see two . "Why are they in the ?" asks .

owls

tree

Lofty

"They live there," says .

Bob

"I wouldn't want to live in a ," says . "Too high!"

tree

Lofty

They see some rabbits hopping down a hole.

rabbits

"They live in the hole," says . "One, two, three, four, five."

Bob

20

"I wouldn't want to live in a hole," says Lofty. "Too dark!"

They notice lots of little bumps near the tree.
"They are mole hills," says Bob.
" moles live in the ground."
"I wouldn't want to live in the ground,"
says Lofty. "Too scary!"

Scoop digs, and finds a nest of mice.
"Ooo, no," says Lofty
"Mmmmmmmice!"
"The nest is their home," says Bob.
"We'll move the tree when they have
gone."

"I'm glad I live in the yard!" says Lofty.

21

Count with Lofty

"Can you help me count the animals?
Count, and write the number in each box."

Spud the Ghost

"Hee, hee! I love playing tricks on people! Here's a story about the time I dressed up as a scary ghost …"

One day, Spud was racing along the lane when Muck beeped loudly at him. **"BEEEEP!"**

"Aaargh!" cried Spud. Muck's beep gave him such a fright that he jumped into the air, and ended up in the hedge!

"Sorry, Spud, I didn't mean to make you jump. Bye!" said Muck, and he rushed off.

"Oww!" cried Spud, rubbing his nose.

Then he found a sheet on a hedge and it gave him an idea. "It's Muck's turn to get a fright now," he said as he put the sheet over his head. "From Spud the ghost!"

"**Woooooh!**" he called.

"**Ark! Ark!**" croaked Squawk the crow when he saw Spud.

Spud was under the sheet, so he couldn't see Squawk. "**Aaargh!**" he said. "What's that? It sounds like a big scary monster!"

He tried to run off, but he tripped on the sheet and pulled it off his head. When he saw Squawk he said, "Oh, it's only you! I wasn't really scared, you know!"

He put the sheet back over his head and went back to pretending to be a ghost. Then he heard rustling noises. "**Aaargh!**" cried Spud. "It sounds like a big bad wolf!"

He ran away, but the sheet got caught on a fence and came off.

Three moles were watching him.

"Oh, hello," said Spud. "Er … I was only pretending to be scared, you know."

It was getting dark, and Muck was near a high hedge. He was getting scared. "Ooh," he said. "I don't like the dark. Maybe if I whistle I'll be OK." So he whistled as loudly as he could.

Spud was on the other side of the hedge and he heard the whistling. "Oh, no!" he whispered to himself. "What if it's a real ghost? I know, I'll scare him before he scares me!"

So Spud waited, then he jumped out. "**BOO!**"

"**Aaaaargh!**" screamed Muck, so loudly that Spud ran off in fright – and bumped into a tree! He slid to the ground and his sheet fell off again.

"It's you, Spud!" said Muck. "I'm sorry about beeping you earlier on."

"And I'm sorry I tried to scare you just now," said Spud. "But why are you here?"

"I'm helping Farmer Pickles look for his sheets. They blew off the washing line."

Just then Farmer Pickles arrived. He pointed to the sheet Spud had been wearing. "You found my best sheet, Spud!" he said. "Well done!"

Spud rubbed his sore head. "Er … yes … er … Spud's on the job!" he said.

"I think you deserve some hot chocolate and cake as a reward," said Farmer Pickles.

Spud suddenly felt better. A **lot** better. "Yes, I think I can manage a small cake …" he laughed.

Ghosts!

"It's fun dressing up and pretending to be a ghost. Who can you see on these pages? Point, and say their names."

Favourite Things

Here are lists of Bob and Wendy's favourite things. Why don't you make a list of things you like?

FAVOURITE THINGS	BOB	WENDY
friend	Wendy	Bob
colour	blue	green
pets	Pilchard and Finn	Bob's pets, Pilchard and Finn
food	cream cake	chocolate cake
hobby	bird watching	painting and gardening
pop star	Lennie Lazenby	Lennie Lazenby
sport	tennis	football

Wendy's Quiz

"I know Bob and the team very well, but what do you know about them? Try answering these questions. Do you know the answers to all 8?"

1. Which of the machines is Bird's best friend?

2. What is the name of Bob's goldfish?

3. Whose dog is Scruffty?

4. What is Muck afraid of?

5. What kind of animal is Lofty most afraid of?

6. Where does Travis live?

7. What job does Mr Bentley do?

8. What is Spud's job?

Answers: 1 Roley, 2 Finn, 3 Farmer Pickles, 4 the dark, 5 mice, 6 on the farm, 7 he's a building inspector, 8 he's a scarecrow, he scares birds away

Roley and the Rock Star

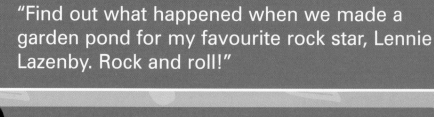
"Find out what happened when we made a garden pond for my favourite rock star, Lennie Lazenby. Rock and roll!"

It was a busy summer morning in the yard. Wendy, Muck and Lofty were loading up the tools they needed to build a nature trail.

"We're going to put these signposts up to show people where they can see plants and animals," Wendy told Muck and Lofty.

Bob came out. "Phew! It's hot today!" he said.

He had a different job for Dizzy, Scoop and Roley to do.

"We're going to build a pond in Lennie Lazenby's garden," Bob told them.

"Lennie Lazenby!" cried Roley. "He's the singer with The Lazers, my top band!"

"**Can we fix it?**" cried Scoop.

"**Yes we can!**" the team cried as they left the yard.

Wendy, Lofty and Muck arrived at the woods. Wendy looked at a map of the nature trail. "This is where it starts," she said.

She dug a hole for the first signpost, and Lofty lifted it into place.

A little duckling came out of the bushes and said, "**QUACK!**" to Lofty!

"**Oooooo, nooooooo!**" he said, shaking with fright.

"What was that noise?" asked Wendy. But the duckling had gone.

"It was a great big … er … quacking thing!" said Lofty. "It scared me!"

"A duck?" said Wendy.

"I can't see any ducks," said Muck. "You must be dreaming, Lofty!"

As they moved along the trail, Lofty kept looking into the bushes.

"What are you looking for?" asked Muck.

"Er … you know," Lofty whispered. "Quacking things!"

Just then, two little ducklings waddled out of a bush. "**Quack, QUACK!**"

"Ooooo-er!" said Lofty.

"You were right about the ducks," said Wendy. "But I wonder why they're so far away from a pond?"

Then another duckling appeared – on the end of Lofty's crane! "Ooooooo, no-no-no-no!" he cried. "Take it away!"

The duckling flew down and waddled into the bushes. "**Quack!**"

Wendy tried to make Lofty feel better. "You silly billy," she told him. "The little ducklings are more frightened of a big machine like you than you are of them!"

"But I won't hurt them!" he said, looking surprised.

"I know, Lofty," said Wendy. "Let's take them back to their pond."

Meanwhile, at Lennie Lazenby's house, Scoop was digging a hole for the pond in the garden. Roley and Dizzy danced around to the pop music coming from Lennie's house.

"I'm going to use these rocks to build a rockery," said Bob. "So I need some cement, please, Dizzy."

Dizzy started mixing as fast as she could. "Coming up!"

"Roley, will you roll the ground flat, please?" asked Bob.

"OK, Bob," said Roley, still dancing. "Rock and roll!"

Lennie came out of the house

to watch Bob turn on the fountain in the pond. It sent jets of water up into the air. "Groovy!" said Lennie.

In the woods, Wendy, Muck and Lofty followed the ducklings to their pond. But when they arrived, it was just a muddy hole.

"The hot weather has dried up all the water," said Wendy. "The ducklings can't stay here. They need a new home. Let's round them up, team."

Muck scooped up the ducklings, then they all set off to meet Bob at Lennie Lazenby's house.

"Look what we found!" said Wendy. "Ducklings! Their pond has dried up, and we can't find the mother duck." She looked at the pond. "Er, could we put them in your pond, Lennie?"

"Sure!" said Lennie. "Ducks are … like … really groovy!"

The ducklings jumped into the pond and Lofty rolled over to watch them swimming around. One of them jumped out and looked at him. "**QUACK!**"

"He's saying THANK YOU," said Muck.

"He's not scared of me any more!" said Lofty.

Just then, the mother duck waddled across the grass and jumped into the pond!

"**Quack, quack, quack!**" said the ducklings.

Bob laughed. "She must have been looking for a new pond, and now she's found one!"

Lennie played his new song for them.

"Rock and roll!" said Roley.

"**Quack, quack, quack!**" said the ducklings.

Rock and Roll

"It was fun when I took some time off from building and became a pop star. But it was still hard work! This is a page from my scrap book."

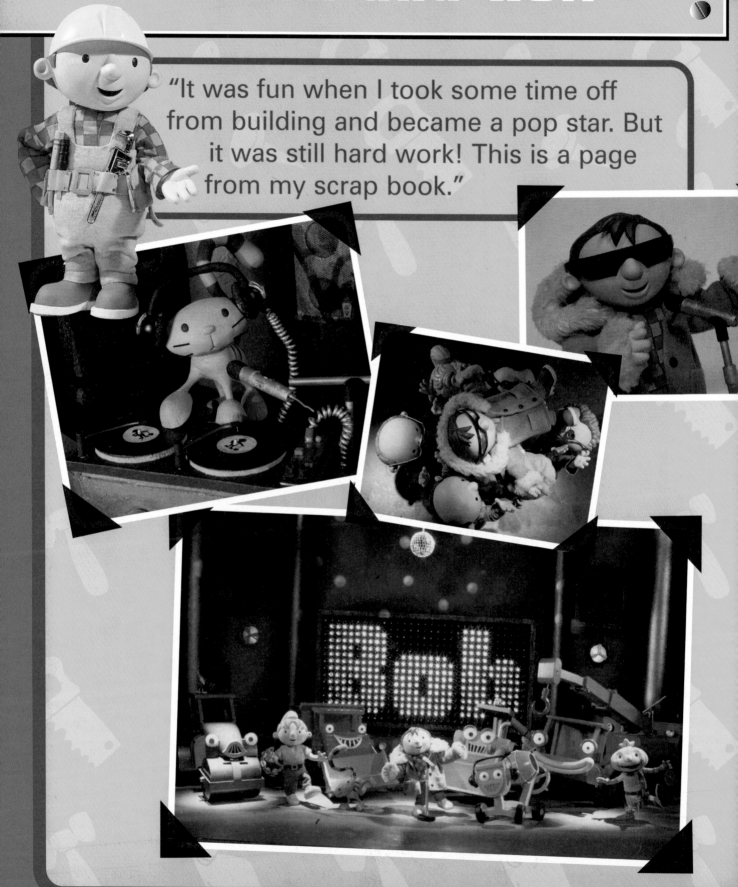

"Why don't you sing along to our song? It's fun!"

Can we fix it?

Bob the Builder, can we fix it?
Bob the Builder, yes we can.

Scoop, Muck and Dizzy and Roley too,
Lofty and Wendy, join the crew,
Bob and the gang have so much fun,
Working together, they get the job done.

Bob the Builder, can we fix it?
Bob the Builder, yes we can.

Time to get busy, such a lot to do,
Building and fixing till it's as good as new,
Bob and the gang make a really good sound,
Working all day till the sun goes down.

Bob the Builder, can we fix it?
Bob the Builder, yes we can.

Digging and mixing, having so much fun,
Working together, they get the job done.

Bob the Builder, can we fix it?
Bob the Builder, yes we can.

This song appears on Bob's new album. It's in the shops this autumn!

hoot!

ark!

squeak!

ruff!

"Lofty discovered that even though ducks are very noisy, they are not scary at all. Point to an animal, say its name, then point to the noise it makes, and say it as loudly as you can. Have fun!"

toot!

quack!

miaow!

Scruffty's Bath Time

Read this story about Scruffty. The little pictures will help you.

Scruffty is digging. He's covered in mud

"Time for a ," says .

bath

Farmer Pickles

But hates having a  .

Scruffty

bath

"Ruff!" says, and runs away!

Scruffty

 can't catch  .

Travis

Scruffty

He hides behind the shed.

Then he runs into and knocks him over.

Spud

 catches him and puts him in the !

bath

Spud

 jumps out and shakes. Now

Scruffty

Spud

is wet!

 dries them with towels.

Farmer Pickles

He has something for them.

There's a doughnut for and a

Spud

bone for  !

Scruffty

"Thanks!" says .

Spud

"Ruff!" says  .

Scruffty

Spot the Difference

"I really like doing puzzles. You can do this one with me. Look carefully at the two pictures on these pages."

"They look the same, but there are five things that are different in the second picture. Can you find all five and point to them?"

Scarecrow Dizzy

"When Farmer Pickles asked me to put up a new shed while Wendy painted the farmhouse white it sounded like a nice easy job. But that was before Spud decided to help ..."

"What jobs do we have today?" the machines asked Bob and Wendy one morning.

"Well, I'll be painting Farmer Pickles's farmhouse," said Wendy. "Lofty, I'll need you to help with the higher bits."

"As long as they're not TOO high!" said Lofty.

"And Farmer Pickles has asked me to build him a new shed," said Bob. "Scoop, Muck and Dizzy, I'll need your help."

"Do you want to come too?" Dizzy whispered to Pilchard. "Come on, hide in my mixer."

When everything was ready, Bob said, "Come on, teams, let's go!"

"**Can we fix it?**" said Scoop.

"**Yes we can!**" said the others.

"Er ... yeah, I think so," said Lofty.

Wendy was painting the farmhouse wall white when Spud came along. "Can I help?" he asked.

Lofty wasn't sure. Spud was always playing tricks and being naughty. "Oooo," he said. "I don't like it, Wendy."

Wendy looked hard at Spud. "Spud will be extra careful, I'm sure. Won't you, Spud?"

"I'll be really careful," said Spud. "Promise!"

Spud got to work painting – but he painted the ladder instead of the wall!

"Perhaps you should stop painting and pass me a tin of paint, please, Spud," said Wendy patiently.

Spud gave Lofty a new tin of paint to pass to Wendy, and she started painting. But the paint was red, not white!

"Don't you like it, Wendy?" said Spud with a cheeky grin.

At the other end of the farm, Scoop was soon hard at work loading Muck with earth.

Bob was going to put a sack of cement into Dizzy when out jumped Pilchard. "**Miaow!**"

"What are you doing here?" asked Bob. "I'll have to take you back to the yard when we've laid this cement."

When Dizzy had mixed the cement, Bob smoothed it out for the shed base. He didn't notice a family of mice poking their heads out of a nearby hedge. Pilchard jumped at them and they ran through Bob's legs towards the wet cement. "Look out!" called Bob.

Dizzy stopped the mice, but she couldn't stop herself, and she skidded across the cement! "Sorry, Bob!"

"It's all right, Dizzy," said Bob. "I'll make it smooth again, then I'll go and get the shed with Travis. We'll take Pilchard with us. You can guard the cement while it sets."

But as soon as Bob had gone, Squawk the crow arrived. Dizzy tried to scare him away, but he took no notice. "Will you keep off the cement if I give you a ride in my mixer?" asked Dizzy.

Squawk nodded his head. "Ark!"

"Come on, then," said Dizzy. **"Vroom! Nee-naw, nee-naw!"**

When Bob and Travis got back with the shed, poor Dizzy was still giving Squawk a ride. She was very tired.

When Squawk saw Bob he flew off. "I was trying to keep him off the cement," said Dizzy. "But I think I'm better at mixing things than I am at scaring birds."

Just then, Bob's mobile phone rang. It was Wendy. "I'm glad you rang," said Bob. "I need Lofty to help with the shed."

"And I need some help with the painting," said Wendy. "Spud's better at scaring crows than painting!"

"Well, a scarecrow is just what I need," said Bob. "I think we should swap helpers."

Spud rushed off to help Bob, and Dizzy set off to help Wendy. They met on the lane.

"Can't stop!" said Spud. "I've got birds to scare!"

"And I've got some mixing to do!" said Dizzy.

The farmhouse looked a mess. There were bits of white wall and bits of red wall.

But Dizzy had an idea. "If we mix white and red, we can paint the walls PINK!"

"Clever Dizzy!" said Wendy.

The painting was soon finished, and Farmer Pickles was very pleased with his pink walls.

"Right, Lofty!" said Wendy. "Let's go and help Bob with the shed."

Scruffty ran along behind them. "**Ruff! Ruff!**"

When they arrived, Pilchard was chasing the mice again, so Scruffty joined in and chased after Pilchard!

"Ooooo," said Lofty. "I don't like them! I don't like them!"

"**Miaow!**"

"**Ruff!**"

"**Squeak! Squeak!**"

The mice ran round and round, and then straight up Spud's trouser leg! "Owww!" he cried. "Get off!"

The mice were very tickly, and Spud ran off, waving his arms around. Pilchard and Scruffty ran off after him.

Soon Squawk the crow joined the chase, too.

"**HELP!**" said Spud.

"Right, Lofty, the mice have gone," said Bob. "Let's get this shed up."

"Can we paint it, Bob?" said Dizzy.

Wendy smiled. "Yes, let's. There's lots of paint left over!"

Soon the new PINK shed was ready. "Brilliant!" cried Dizzy.

"There is one piece missing from each of these jigsaw pictures. Which of the little pictures will complete the big picture?

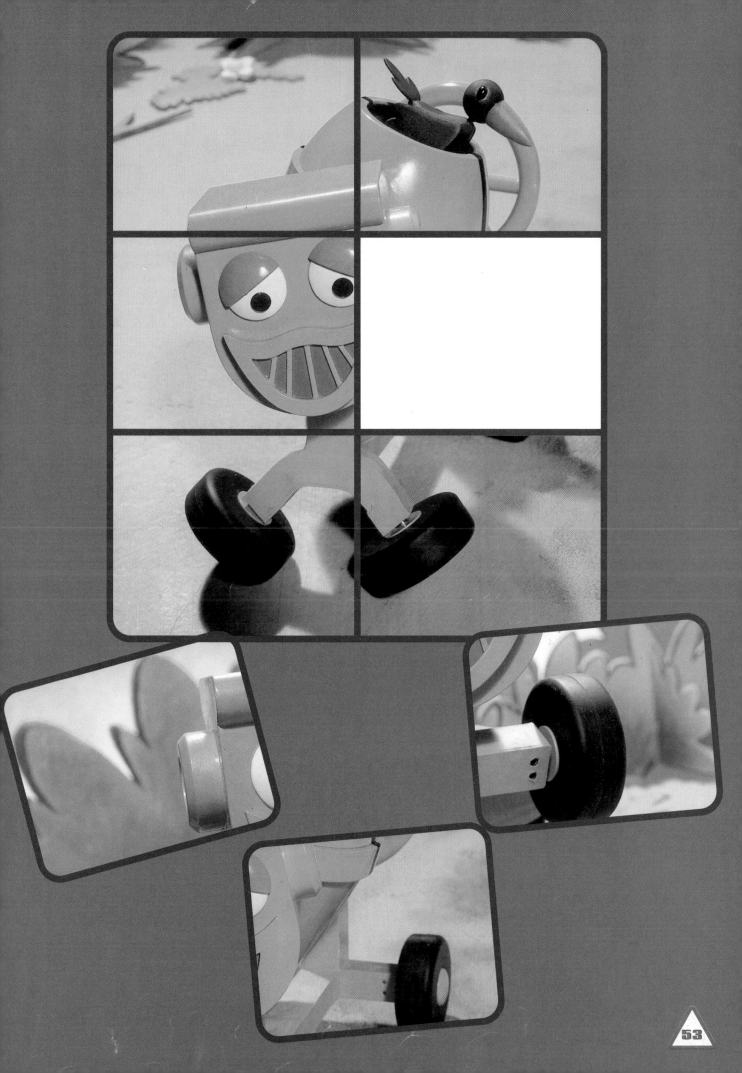

The Christmas Tree

"We all love Christmas. It's a very special time for sharing. And this year we all worked together to make it extra special."

One Christmas, Farmer Pickles told Bob that he could have an extra large tree from the farm.

When Bob, Scoop, Lofty and Muck got to the farm there was snow on the ground.

There were lots and lots of fir trees. "Which one is it?" said Bob.

Just then, Spud jumped out.

"Spud's on the job!" he said. "I'll show you. It's the one on the edge of the field over there."

Scoop used his snowplough to move the snow so that Lofty could get close and pull up the tree. He did it very gently so that he didn't harm the tree's roots.

Muck helped by moving the soil and earth away. He liked that job because it got him all messy and mucky!

But the tree was very heavy and Lofty had to pull really hard. The team encouraged him. "Come on, Lofty. You can do it!"

"Ooo-er," said Lofty. "Very heavy, very heavy!"

With one big heave, Lofty pulled the tree out of the ground.

"Well done!" said Bob, and they all cheered. "Hooray for Lofty!"

Lofty lifted the tree into Muck's dumper and they set off back to the yard.

"Let's get the tree up before it starts to snow," said Wendy.

"But how are we going to get it to stand up?" asked Dizzy.

"I know," said Wendy, and she showed everyone a shiny red bucket.

Lofty gently lowered the tree into the bucket.

"Perfect!" said Bob. "Now we need to decorate it." He brought out some decorations from the house.

Bob climbed a tall ladder to hang strings of Christmas lights on the tree, and he and Wendy hung shiny baubles and tinsel from the branches.

Lofty brought the presents and put them under the tree.

"That's everything," said Bob. "Well done, team. Now it's time to turn on the lights."

Everyone cheered when the tree was lit up.

But Wendy was frowning.

"What's wrong?" asked Bob. "Don't you like it?"

"Oh, yes," said Wendy, looking at the tree. "But there's still something missing. I just can't think what it is."

Just then Bird arrived and landed on the top of the tree. "**Toot!**" he whistled. "**Toot, toot!**"

"That's it!" cried Wendy. "We need something for the top of the tree!"

Bird picked up something from the decorations box and flew up to the tree again. He put a big shiny silver star right at the top.

When they saw it, everyone cheered again.

"Perfect!" said Bob. "And look – here comes the snow! Happy Christmas, everyone!"

Whose Gift?

"There was a Christmas present for everyone under the Christmas tree – even me! But naughty Spud mixed up the gift tags. Can you untangle the strings to see what we got?"

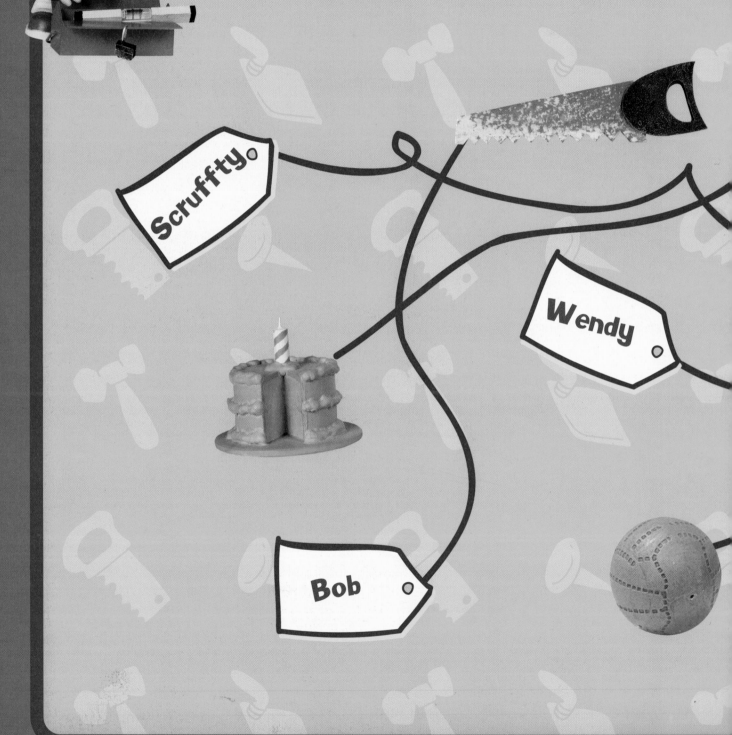

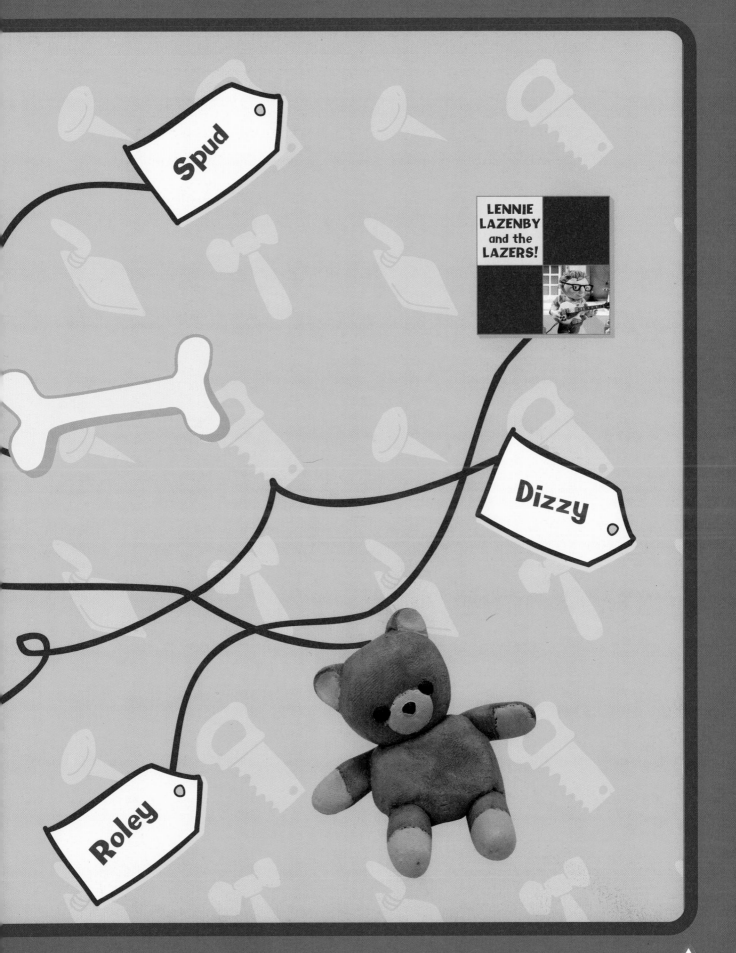

Spud

Dizzy

Roley

LENNIE
LAZENBY
and the
LAZERS!

Competition Time

We've got 4 super Bob the Builder prizes to give away courtesy of VTech Electronics,
2 Bob's Talking Telephone and
2 Bob the Builder's Computer

How to enter:
All you have to do is answer this question:
What is the name of Farmer Pickles's dog?

Write your answer on a postcard or the back of a sealed envelope (don't forget to include your name, address and age) and post to:
Bob the Builder Competition,
Egmont World, Unit 7, Millbank House,
Riverside Park, Bollin Walk,
Wilmslow, Cheshire SK9 1BJ
(Entries to be received by 25 January 2002)

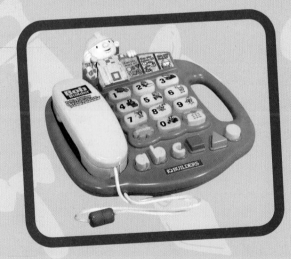

Rules
1 The winners will be chosen at random and notified by post.
2 The judges' decision will be final. No correspondence will be entered into.
3 The winners' names will be made available from Egmont World (on request) after 4 February 2002.
  Please enclose a stamped addressed envelope.
4 Employees (and their relatives) of Egmont World and associated companies are not eligible to enter.
5 Entries are limited to one per person.
6 The competition is open to non-residents of the UK, Channel Islands and Ireland.
7 The publishers reserve the right to vary prizes, subject to availability.
8 The closing date for entries is 25 January 2002.

Have you been surfing yet? No, I don't mean water surfing, I mean surfing the internet! There's a brand new Bob the Builder website packed with exciting and fun games and puzzles to try. You can send emails to me and Wendy, too, and help us finish our jobs. We'd like to hear from you! This is our address.

www.bobthebuilder.com